PREDATOR VS PREY

Lion Vs Gazelle

Mary Meinking

www.raintreepublishers.co.uk
Visit our website to find out
more information about
Raintree books.

To order:
☎ Phone 0845 6044371
🖹 Fax +44 (0) 1865 312263
🖳 Email myorders@raintreepublishers.co.uk

Customers from outside the UK please telephone +44 1865 312262

Raintree is an imprint of Capstone Global Library Limited,
a company incorporated in England and Wales having its
registered office at 7 Pilgrim Street, London, EC4V 6LB
– Registered company number: 6695582

Text © Capstone Global Library Limited 2011
First published in hardback in 2011
The moral rights of the proprietor have
been asserted.

Edited by Rebecca Rissman, Dan Nunn,
    and Catherine Veitch
Designed by Joanna Hinton Malivoire
Levelling by Jeanne Clidas
Picture research by Hannah Taylor
Production by Victoria Fitzgerald
Originated by Capstone Global Library
Printed and bound in China by CTPS

ISBN 978 1 406 21864 0
14 13 12 11 10
10 9 8 7 6 5 4 3 2 1

British Library Cataloguing in Publication Data
Meinking, Mary.
Lion vs gazelle. -- (Predator vs prey)
591.5'3-dc22
A full catalogue record for this book is available from the
British Library.

Acknowledgements
We would like to thank the following for permission
to reproduce photographs: Alamy Images pp. 20 (©
Gary Dublanko), 21 (© Philip Dalton), 22 (© Steve Bloom
Images), 27 (© Bill Gozansky); ardea.com p. 18 (©
Ferrero-Labat); FLPA pp. 8 (Jurgen & Christine Sohns), 10
(Martin B Withers), 14 (Minden Pictures/Mitsuaki Iwago),
23 (Michael Gore), 25 (Ariadne Van Zandbergen), 29
(Malcolm Schuyl); Getty Images p. 9 (Joseph Van Os);
istockphoto pp. 6 (© Carl Fourie), 11 (© brytta), 24 (©
Britta Kasholm-Tengve), 26 (© Peter Malsbury); naturepl
pp. 13 (Francois Savigny), 15 (Peter Blackwell), 16 (Tony
Heald); Photolibrary pp. 4 (Peter Arnold Images/ Martin
Harvey), 5 (Oxford Scientific/ David W Breed), 7 (age
fotostock/ Werner Bollmann), 12 (Birgit Koch), 17 (Fritz
Poelking), 28 (Oxford Scientific/ Elliott Neep); Science
Photo Library p. 19 (William Ervin).

Cover photographs of an African lion reproduced with
permission of Photolibrary (Oxford Scientific/ David
W Breed), and a Thompson's gazelle reproduced with
permission of Alamy Images (© Balman Photography).

We would like to thank Michael Bright for his invaluable
help in the preparation of this book.

Every effort has been made to contact copyright holders
of material reproduced in this book. Any omissions will
be rectified in subsequent printings if notice is given to
the publisher.

Some words are shown in bold, **like this**. You can find
out what they mean by looking in the glossary.

Contents

Claws vs horns

Claws rip! Horns stab! Two animals meet on a dry **plains** battleground! Here is a frightening beast, the lion. It's up against a bouncing challenger, the gazelle.

gazelle

lion

5

These **competitors** live in Africa's **grasslands**. Both have strengths that will help them in this battle.

PREDATOR
African **lioness**

LENGTH: 3 metres

WEIGHT: 136 kilograms

HEIGHT: 1 metre

Key

where African lions and Thomson's gazelles live

PREY
Thomson's gazelle

LENGTH: 0.9 metres

WEIGHT: 29 kilograms

HEIGHT: 0.7 metres

Africa

Girl power

Around 10 to 30 lions live in a group called a **pride**. Most are **lionesses** from the same family. When the lionesses hunt together, they catch more **prey**.

mane

DID YOU KNOW?

There are usually one or two male lions in each pride. They do not hunt with the group. Their big **manes** would give them away if they tried to hide!

9

Super senses

The gazelle has great **vision**. But when it is in tall grass it cannot see its enemies. It uses its excellent senses of smell and hearing instead. Staying in a **herd** means there are more noses and ears to smell and hear **prey**!

DID YOU KNOW?

The gazelle is a tan colour. This helps it blend in with the dry grass.

Who's hungry?

Lions are **carnivores**, or animals that eat meat. There are many mouths to feed in each **pride**. So the **lionesses** need to hunt and kill enough meat for everyone.

DID YOU KNOW?
Most lions eat 7 kilograms of meat a day! That's like eating 60 hamburgers every day!

Stalking game

From a hilltop, four **lionesses** watch a **herd** of gazelles. They're looking for a young, old, or hurt gazelle. They are easier to catch.

The lioness can smell the gazelle is near.

They spot one! The lionesses split up. Two lionesses circle around the other side of the gazelle herd. They sneak towards the **prey**.

15

They creep closer. The plan is for one **lioness** to scare the gazelle towards the other two. When the lioness is near the gazelle, she charges at it.

DID YOU KNOW? Lions have soft pads on the bottom of their feet. These pads help them **stalk prey** quietly. It is like wearing trainers.

A gazelle sees the **lioness** coming. It **stots**, or jumps straight up. This tells the lioness the gazelle is too healthy to catch. The stotting also tells the other gazelles that danger is nearby. The gazelles run in every direction.

DID YOU KNOW?
A gazelle can jump up to
three metres high. That's as
high as four school desks
on top of each other!

The **lioness** runs after the closest gazelle. The gazelle starts running. The lioness's thick muscular legs pound the dry ground trying to catch it. It keeps low so the gazelle cannot see it.

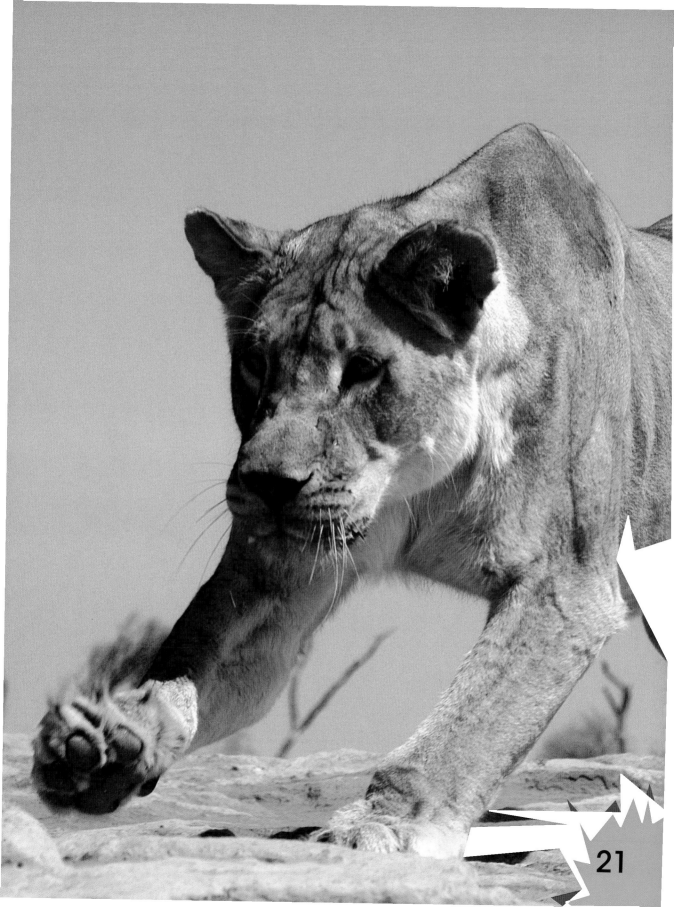

The **lioness** cannot run far. She needs to catch the gazelle soon. She chases it at 58 kilometres per hour. That is faster than a car goes in a town!

The gazelle runs in a **zigzag,** or Z-shaped pattern. It's trying to lose the **lioness.** The lioness stays with the gazelle for several minutes. But soon the gazelle goes one way as the lioness goes the other. The lioness loses the gazelle in the tall grass.

DID YOU KNOW?
Lions do not always catch their food. Often they will steal **prey** from other animals.

And the winner is...

...the gazelle! The gazelle is not big enough to fight off enemies. So its best defence is to run! Being able to run fast and turn quickly saved it from being the **lioness's** next meal.

What are the odds?

Because **lionesses** are slow, they rely on teamwork. What one lioness misses, another can catch. So lions make great team players!

DID YOU KNOW?

A lioness hunting alone only catches **prey** once every seven tries. But when she hunts with others, they catch prey every three tries.

Glossary

carnivore animal that eats meat

grasslands land where mostly grasses grow

herd group of animals living together

lioness female lion

mane long fur that grows around the head of male lions

plain flat land with few trees

predator animal that hunts other animals

prey animal that is hunted by other animals for food

pride group of lions, usually one or two males and several females with their cubs

stalk sneak up on prey

stotting jumping high with stiff legs

vision eyesight

zigzag several sharp turns to change direction

Find out more

Books

Encyclopedia of *Animals* (Dorling Kindersley, 2006)

Watching Lions in Africa, Louise and Richard Spilsbury (Heinemann Library, 2007)

Websites

http://animals.nationalgeographic.com/ animals/mammals/gazelle/
Find out more about Thomson's gazelles on this website.

http://kids.nationalgeographic.com/kids/ animals/creaturefeature/lion
On this website you can learn about lions, watch videos, and print off collector's cards.

http://www.bbc.co.uk/bigcat/
Visit the Big Cat website to watch videos and find out about prides of lions living in Africa.

Index